*"Every child comes with the message that God is
not yet discouraged in humanity"*
(Rabindranath Tagore)

Mommy Please Read This

The FACTS About Child Sexual Abuse

TROY D. TIMMONS, M.ED., L.P.C.

Mommy Please Read This
The FACTS About Child Sexual Abuse

Published by
Thomas, Grace & Mae Publishing
United States of America
©2010 by Troy D. Timmons

No part of this publication may be reproduced, stored in a retrieval system, or transmitted, in any form or by any means—electronic, mechanical, photocopying, recording, or otherwise—without prior written permission.

The website addresses recommended throughout this book are offered as a resource to you. These websites are not intended in any way to be or imply an endorsement on the part of Thomas, Grace & Mae Publishing, nor do we vouch for their content for the life of this book.

ALL RIGHTS RESERVED

Printed in the United States of America
Cover Design by Troy D. Timmons
Cover photo by Carol McKinney

Library of Congress Cataloging-in-Publication Data
Timmons, Troy D.
Mommy, please read this: the facts about child sexual abuse / Troy D. Timmons
   ISBN: 978-0-692-00983-3

For Kids Everywhere

Author's Note

The names of the people described in this book have been changed to protect their privacy. This publication is designed to provide accurate information in regard to the subject matter covered. This publication is sold with the understanding that it is not a substitute for professional services. If expert assistance or counseling is needed, the services of a competent professional should be sought.

Table of Contents

Foreword		*xv*
Acknowledgements		*xvii*
Introduction		*xix*
CHAPTER ONE	*What Is Child Sexual Abuse?*	27
CHAPTER TWO	*Who Is at Risk?*	37
CHAPTER THREE	*Why Survivors Don't Tell*	51
CHAPTER FOUR	*Portrait of the Molester*	61
CHAPTER FIVE	*How Molesters Operate*	71
CHAPTER SIX	*Responding Appropriately to Child Sexual Abuse*	81
CHAPTER SEVEN	*Preventing Child Sexual Abuse*	91
Conclusion		*109*
About the Author		*111*
Resources		*113*
Endnotes		*121*

*"See that you do not despise one of these little ones.
For I tell you that in heaven their angels always see the
face of my Father who is in heaven."
(Matthew 18:10)*

Foreword

I have wrestled with the idea of writing a book about preventing and responding appropriately to child sexual abuse for several years. An encounter with a particular little girl and her mother helped me take up the challenge.

Audrey and her sister had been adopted after enduring several years of abuse and neglect. I loaned their adoptive mother an excellent book about how to respond to child sexual abuse, and we agreed to discuss the material at our next appointment. When she returned, however, Mom had not read the book. "I couldn't get past the title. It's just too scary." Here was a nurturing, educated, loving mother telling me the title of the book I had suggested so disturbed her that she found it unreadable.

There are numerous books about child sexual abuse available to the reader. Most include an abundance of research and suggestions for preventing and responding appropriately to sexual abuse. Does the world really need another book on the subject? Obviously, I believe the answer is yes. Not because the available books are poorly written or provide bad information, but because

Mommy, Please Read This

parents are not reading them unless they have to.

So, are there millions of irresponsible parents burying their heads in the sand on this issue? Some may suggest this is exactly the problem. I tend to believe, however, that child sexual abuse is simply "too scary" for most of us to digest, unless we have to. When was the last time you picked up a book on pancreatic cancer? Probably never, unless the subject has been forced upon you or a loved one.

The difference is this. Thirty-three percent of girls are subjected to sexual abuse before their 18th birthday. Sixteen percent of boys are in the same boat. Simply put, this means you already know a child who has been or will be sexually abused. So, regardless of our reasons for not talking or reading about this issue, millions of children need us to face it and learn enough to help them.

My hope in writing this book is to provide you with the essential information on a disgusting subject in an approachable format, one that you won't mind reading at your favorite coffee shop or sharing with your closest friend. If you are reading these words, then it seems you have gotten past the title. Thank you and please read on.

Acknowledgements

Thanks to Tammy, Beck, Ava, and Lily for affording me the time to write and encouraging me throughout the process. I am blessed indeed.

Thanks to the numerous friends and colleagues who shared their time and ideas in developing, editing, and reviewing this book. A thank-you also to the members of the multidisciplinary teams across America that passionately help children every day, and the sex offender treatment providers for taking on the challenge.

I want to give special thanks to Regina Hamner of BookMasters. Your honest, gentle approach was both refreshing and helpful for me as a first-time author.

Lastly, thanks to Bill O'Hanlon, psychotherapist, author, and endlessly unselfish creative mind, for encouraging me to practice, speak, and write.

Introduction

I am writing this because I have to. For the past 19 years, I have worked—initially as a probation officer and currently as a therapist—with both victims and offenders of sexual abuse. I have interviewed and treated hundreds of child molesters and sexual abuse survivors. I have testified in trial after trial as an expert witness on child sexual abuse and those who perpetrate it. I want you to hear and understand what I have learned from working with victims and offenders.

I have to write this book because our children, our families, our communities, and our society desperately need the facts about child sexual abuse.

I have to write this book because mothers need to know who is most likely to be victimized and who is most likely to abuse. Of course, fathers need this information as well, but I believe it is Mom who can and will have an impact on the issue of child sexual abuse.

This crucial information is based on what therapists, police, prosecuting attorneys, trauma teams, victims' advocates, teachers, social workers, etc. see on a daily basis. What these foot soldiers see of child sexual abuse is different from what you see reported in the media. That is why I have to write this book.

Having recently read books by Malcolm Gladwell, Mitch Albom, Randy Pausch, and Daniel Gilbert, I keep asking myself, "What am I doing writing a book?" Then I meet another victim of sexual abuse or another offender who made such a destructive choice, and I write some more.

My goal is to provide a clear picture of the risk a child faces concerning sexual abuse. I have purposefully provided essential information, which is easy to read, and relatively free from therapy jargon and psychobabble. I want to tie essential information together with true accounts from years of working within the child sexual abuse arena. My goal is to produce a fact-filled book about child sexual abuse that will assist you in keeping kids safe.

My goal is to help you see who is most likely to sexually abuse your child, give you a window into the molester's mind, and help you know how to respond appropriately if your child and your family deal with the trauma of child sexual abuse.

I do not intend to frighten or offend. The stories of hurt, healing, and hope on the pages that follow are true, although the names have been changed for obvious reasons. I think your beliefs will be challenged. I hope you will assess the risk we are all facing and pass along the facts to responsible adults in your life as we protect our most precious gift—our children.

"Sexual abuse is an assault on the soul."
(Cloe Madanes)

Published by
Thomas, Grace, & Mae
2010

Mommy Please Read This

The FACTS About Child Sexual Abuse

TROY D. TIMMONS, M.ED., L.P.C.

Chapter One:
What Is Child Sexual Abuse?

But whoever causes one of these little ones who believe in Me to stumble, it is better for him that a heavy millstone be hung around his neck, and that he be drowned in the depth of the sea.
(Matthew 18:6) [i]

Sexual abuse is an issue that splits families and communities in half.

As I write this book, a local high school teacher is under investigation for possible inappropriate conduct with students. The local newspaper ran the story with an abundance of information about the allegations, the school's response, the district's decision to dismiss the teacher, and the results of the mediated agreement.

I know nothing about the matter, other than what was reported in the newspaper.

I have heard, however, comments from people on both sides of the guilt/innocence coin. As usual, the accused teacher seems to have supporters and critics. Many have voiced their staunch support for him. Others have already condemned him. Both groups are acting prematurely, in part, due to differences of opinion concerning what constitutes sexual abuse.

Sexual abuse divides families and communities.

Another example illustrating this division involved a male high school coach accused of sexual activity with a 16-year-old female student.

Before, during, and after his placement on probation, the high school coach denied having an inappropriate relationship with the girl. His supporters included faculty members, current and former students, members of his church community, and his family. Their strong, unyielding allegiance was related to his good reputation, skill as an educator, and overall appearance of normal.

His critics, however, were confident the allegations were true. Like his supporters, this group consisted of current and former students, professional colleagues, and community members. Like his supporters', the critics' minds were made up.

After a brief period on probation, the coach was accused of attempting to contact his victim. This resulted in his probation being revoked. I testified at the revocation hearing.

When testifying, witnesses are usually not allowed into the courtroom until they take the witness stand. The hearing lasted well into the night. I took the witness stand at about 10:00 p.m.

As I entered the large courtroom, divided down the

middle by a single aisle, I was reminded of being at a Baptist wedding—the groom's family seated on the right and the bride's family seated on the left. Except now, the coach's supporters packed one side of the courtroom and his critics, the other. Literally, there were no available seats, and media crews were set up in the hallway.

After my testimony, the state rested its case, and I was released. Defense counsel announced that the coach would testify. He took the stand just before midnight, speaking to an exhausted crowd of friends and critics, court personnel, family members, and the weirdly curious.

I stood at the back of the courtroom as the accused educator tearfully admitted committing the acts alleged against him. He was guilty, and he had lied about it. He was apologetic and asked for the Court's understanding. The coach's admissions validated his critics' beliefs.

His supporters, however, heard for the first time that they had been deceived by a man they held in high esteem. I watched as his family cried and normal, intelligent men and women, young to old, tried to make sense of what they were hearing. Several exchanged glances with each other, asking, "What did he say?" One man, obviously angry that he had been duped, stormed from the courtroom.

What I saw in this case, as in so many others, is sexual abuse's ability to tear families and communities apart. Some of this relates to how we want to see the people in our lives. Some of this relates to our struggle to understand and agree on what constitutes sexual abuse.

From state to state, for example, laws, age of consent, penalties, and definitions of sexual acts involving children vary. As a parent, I do not care about the subtle differences of definition, and I doubt that you do, either. When a child is sexually abused, a horrific assault on many levels is taking place. Child sexual abuse is never justified, never excusable, and never without harm to the victim, family, and community.

Child Sexual Abuse Defined

In this book, child sexual abuse (CSA) is defined as *"[a] behavior between an adult and child, or in some cases, an older child and younger child, that is intended to sexually please one or both of the parties."*

The American Medical Association defines child sexual abuse as *"the engagement of a child in sexual activities for which the child is developmentally unprepared and cannot give informed consent. Child sexual abuse is characterized by deception, force or coercion."* [ii]

Generation FIVE, a social awareness organization that is working to end child sexual abuse in the next five generations, provides this excellent overview of child sexual abuse:

> *Child sexual abuse (CSA) is the overarching term for a huge, complicated, personally and so-*

> *cially damaging issue. At the base of child sexual abuse is the sexual use of a child by someone with more power. It is the use of a child to satisfy the offender's own needs for power or sex, disregarding the child's needs and sending a message that the child's wishes about his or her own body are unimportant.[iii]*

Generally, it is illegal for an adult to have sexual contact with a minor or for an older child to have sexual contact with a younger child. Teenagers, for example, are prohibited from having sexual contact with preteens due to differences in age and maturation.

Child sexual abuse can include non-touching and touching behaviors. Examples of non-touching abuse include the following:

Voyeurism - secretly watching a person to obtain sexual pleasure. The key to true voyeurism is secrecy. Peeping Toms, hidden cameras, and holes drilled in the locker room ceiling are examples of voyeurism.

Exhibitionism - exposing one's genitals (privates) to an unsuspecting person. The "flasher" is the obvious example. Exhibitionism can constitute child sexual abuse when the victim is a child, even if the act is not a surprise to the victim. I have interviewed several offenders who frequently exposed themselves to children in their care because it was sexually arousing to the adult, served to desensitize the child to sexuality, or both.

Exposure to pornography - many offenders use pornography to introduce and desensitize children to sex. Magazines, television, photographs, and, most notably, the Internet allow offenders numerous opportunities to subject a child to pornography. Often played off by the offender as an honest mistake, knowingly and intentionally exposing a child to pornography is child sexual abuse. Interestingly, it is not universally agreed that showing pornography to a child constitutes abuse. In Texas, for example, an outdated law allows for a parent or guardian to show a child in his or her care pornography for "sexual education."

Examples of child sexual abuse that involve physical contact can range from touching a child's private areas (breast, buttocks, penis, vagina, anus) to penetration acts such as anal, oral, or vaginal sex. Contact offenses can occur whenever touch occurs under or over clothing.

Any behavior that involves either person interacting for sexual pleasure comprises an abusive act. This distinction is important when considering cases in which the offender has encouraged the child to touch or penetrate himself or herself or other children or to touch the offender in private areas. I have interviewed offenders who were careful to not "actually" touch their victims to avoid detection.

What is Child Sexual Abuse?

Child sexual abuse occurs whenever a child is exploited for sexual pleasure. The abuse is not lessened or tempered by the child's involvement (voluntary or coerced). Offenders who believe their victims were the seducers are rationalizing their deviant sexual behavior. These offenders do not recognize that they, not the child, are 100 percent responsible for the abuse.

Often I am asked if the victim ever shares responsibility for the abuse. Example questions and my responses follow:

Q: What about the seductive teenaged girl, dressed like a pop star and obviously sexual? Isn't she at fault, too?
A: No. One hundred percent of the responsibility rests with the offender.
Q: What about the offender who succumbs to the "victim's" advances?
A: One hundred percent of the responsibility lies with the offender. Always.

We must be clear on this point. Children, even older children who may look like young adults, are never responsible for being sexually abused. NEVER.

Think about this. The difference between a child molester and a responsible adult is, when faced with a child who can be easily manipulated or abused, the responsible adult protects the child while seeking help. The molester preys on the vulnerability, sexual curiosity, previous abuse, etc. to meet his or her own agenda—sexual pleasure.

Consider, for example, a married, 35-year-old business owner having sex with a 16-year-old female employee. The girl was sexually active and had developed a reputation for promiscuity. Often, children in this situation are blamed wholly or partially for their abuse. The seduction of the offender may be offered as an excuse—by offenders and their supporters—for the abusive act.

When I hear people blaming the seductive child, I ask if they would take the same position if their partner had sex with their best friend or with a prostitute. The prostitute made a pass at him, after all, and I hear your friend gets around. Does either fact change his or her responsibility in the matter? If we will not make excuses for a person's behavior in these examples, then it is silly and hurtful to apply them in abusive acts against children.

CHAPTER ONE:
WHAT IS CHILD SEXUAL ABUSE?
SUMMARY

- Sexual abuse may occur between an adult and a child or between an older child and a younger child.

- Child sexual abuse can involve non-touching and touching behavior(s).

What is Child Sexual Abuse?

- Child sexual abuse is an abuse of power.
- The child is NEVER to blame in sexual abuse.

Chapter Two: Who Is at Risk?

Epidemic | `epi`demik
Spreading rapidly and extensively by infection and affecting many individuals in an area or a population at the same time: an epidemic outbreak of influenza. Widely prevalent: epidemic discontent. An outbreak of a contagious disease that spreads rapidly and widely. A rapid spread, growth, or development: an unemployment epidemic. [iv]

WHAT ARE THE ODDS?

In 1996, the American Medical Association declared child sexual abuse an epidemic.[v] It is estimated that one of every three girls and one of every six boys will be molested before their 18th birthday. That is hard for me to comprehend, frankly.

Imagine if the American Medical Association announced today that 33 percent of all girls will die of cancer before age 18 and that 16 percent of all boys will be murdered before age 18. Now imagine that, in 90 percent of these horrible events, someone the child knows, loves, and trusts causes the trauma. This is what we are seeing with child sexual abuse.

In a July 2000 study, the U.S. Department of Justice published the following startling findings in its report *Sexual Assault of Young Children as Reported to Law Enforcement: Victim, Incident, and Offender Characteristics:* [vi]

- More than two-thirds (67 percent) of all victims of sexual assault reported to law enforcement agencies were juveniles. More than half of all juvenile victims were under age 12.

- One out of every seven victims of sexual assault (14 percent of all victims) was under age six.

- For victims under age 12, four year olds were at greatest risk of being the victim of a sexual assault.

- The risk of forcible fondling peaks at age four, drops marginally through the pre-teen years, and then increases to its absolute peak for victims at age 13.

The same study revealed important information pertaining to the gender of sexual assault victims:

- Girls were more than six times as likely as boys to be the victims of sexual assaults known to law enforcement agencies. More to the point, 86 percent of all victims of sexual assault were female.

- Sixty-nine percent of victims under age six were girls, compared with 73 percent of victims under the age of 12.

IDENTIFIED RISK MARKERS

According to *Advocates for Youth*, the primary markers for increased risk for child sexual abuse for girls are having few friends, absent or unavailable parents, a stepfather, and conflict with or between parents.[vii]

Other risk factors include physical or mental disability; separate living arrangements from both biological parents; mental illness, alcoholism, or drug abuse in the family; a parent who was physically or sexually abused as a child; and homes with other forms of abuse, prostitution, or transient adults.[viii]

STRANGER DANGER IS **NOT** THE PROBLEM

Numerous studies estimate that a family member or person known to and trusted by the victim and victim's family molests nine out of 10 victims of child sexual abuse.[ix] While there are high profile, horrific cases of child abduction, rape, and murder, the actual number of cases involving strangers is estimated by the FBI to be less than one percent. Overwhelmingly, child sex abuse appears to be a family system (immediate and extended) issue, making incest the most common form of abuse and abuse by strangers the most rare.

In 2002, the National Center for Health Statistics published their findings from a study examining stereotypical kidnappings. The study found that a child was two times more likely to die of influenza or pneumonia, four times more likely to die of heart disease, 17 times more likely to commit suicide, and 100 times more likely to die of an accidental injury than to become a victim of a 'stereotypical type' of abduction. The odds of a child being 'stereotypically' abducted are one in 610,000, the odds of dying in an airplane crash in any given year are one in 310,000 (two times more likely), the odds of being struck by lightning are one in 240,000 (2.5 times more likely), and the odds of a pedestrian being killed by an automobile are one in 47,000 (13 times more likely).

Of the 69,000 child abductions that occurred in 1999, family members perpetrated 82 percent. Friends of the family or other people well known to the children committed another 11.3 percent. [x]

Society has become fixated on stranger abductions and the myth of child abuse happening at the hands of strangers to a degree that we have overlooked the unpleasant truth: the vast majority of child sexual abuse is committed by family members and friends of the family. [xi]

Who poses the greatest risk to your children? The answer is family and friends. Consistently, about 10 percent of molesters report sexually abusing strangers.

According to the Bridge Children's Advocacy Center in my hometown of Amarillo, Texas, family members and friends of the family comprise 99 percent of the child sexual abuse cases investigated in the area. Many people I meet at my seminars on child sexual abuse are surprised to hear these percentages because they have heard so much about "stranger danger" when discussing child sexual abuse. Additional information recently published by the Bridge includes the following: [xii]

- Seventy percent of victims are female.

- Ninety-five percent of sexual offenders are male.

- Thirty-three percent of children interviewed in sexual abuse cases are five years of age and younger.

- Forty-seven percent are six to 12 years of age.

- Twenty percent are 13 to 17 years of age.

In a 2001 landmark study on the demographics of child molesters, Gene Abel, M.D., and Nora Harlow looked closely at the children verified molesters were abusing. Of the 3,952 men who admitted being child molesters, 68 percent reported they had molested a child in their family.

Abel and Harlow also reported that 40 percent of the offenders had molested the children of friends and neighbors; and that nearly 24 percent of the men who were sexually abusing children in their family were also molesting children of friends and neighbors.

Numerous studies point out who is most likely to be a victim of child sexual abuse. Consider these findings reported by Darkness to Light, a national nonprofit organization committed to decreasing child sexual abuse: [xiii]

- The median age for reported abuse is nine years old. [xiv]

- More than 20 percent of children are abused before the age of eight years. [xv]

- Approximately 40 percent are abused by older or larger children whom the victims know. [xvi]

- Approximately 10 percent are abused by strangers. [xvii]

These studies, while having subtle differences in their findings, clearly indicate that those whom children know and trust are abusing them most often. This tells us we have to better know the people spending time with our children.

JAKE AND RUDY

Knowing who is spending time with our children is more difficult in practice than in theory.

Jake and Rudy were best friends and codefendants in a vandalism spree that proved costly for their parents. The teens were referred to an adolescent social skills group I led for a juvenile probation department. Immediately apparent was the boys' close friendship.

Following the weekly adolescent group was the parent group. I met with parents to discuss their children's adjustment, treatment needs, and concerns. Because there were several new families beginning the program, I asked parents to introduce themselves and give a brief description of how they became involved with the juvenile authorities.

Parents were seated in a semicircle just as their children had been in the group before. Jake's father introduced himself first. "Jake is our son. He would not be in this trouble if it had not been for getting involved with some little thug named Rudy."

One after another, parents introduced themselves, explaining their circumstances as requested, until I came to the last set of parents. "I am Eric, and this is my wife, Heather. We're the little thug's parents!"

Amazingly, Jake and Rudy's parents did not know each other. Their children were best friends, spent hours together at each other's homes, smoked marijuana together almost daily, and had even been arrested together. The parents had never spoken to each other, much less met. While this story does not involve sexual abuse, this illustrates a disconnect within families that often occurs. Sex offenders exploit this, as we will discuss in chapter five.

A CONFESSION

My daughter was nine years old. A girl she knew from Sunday school had been calling relentlessly, inviting her to spend the night in her home. After putting the matter off several times, I eventually gave in to the girls' request. A sleepover with a kid from Sunday school sounded good to me.

My wife reminded me that we had not met the girl's parents.

I protested. "I think we met them at church, didn't we?"

Realizing my mistake, I told my daughter we would need to meet her friend's parents before she could go on the sleepover.

My nine year old's reply? "But Dad, her parents are gone for the weekend, and her teenaged brother is in charge. Do you want to meet with him?"

An emerging fact is that teenaged boys commit much of the child sexual abuse perpetrated against children.[xviii] Was I about to place my daughter in harm's way? What is certain is that I may have put her into harm's way by assuming the parents would be home and that their attendance at church was a sufficient test for safety. It is not.

One need not look further than the sex scandals of the church to understand that being religious has no predictive ability whatsoever to identify a molester. Many offenders use religion to suggest they are innocent.

ANSWERED PRAYERS

In 1995, I met a married couple dealing with a sexual abuse accusation within their family. The allegation involved the teenaged stepdaughter making an outcry against her stepfather. Rather than believe and protect the child, the deeply religious parents requested prayers for their family and, specifically, for the "obviously troubled child." The girl's mother described how she and her accused husband stood at the altar of their small church, encircled by the congregation, praying that the truth would be revealed.

Well, let me just say, "Be careful what you ask for." The truth, as it turned out, was made known when the stepfather confessed to sexually abusing his stepdaughter, after months of denying the allegation and after calling on the church to aid his defense.

We think we know the people in our lives. But do we really? Most of the parents I have met would have never allowed their children to be around someone they thought might be an abuser. This speaks to the incredible skill a molester possesses to deceive caregivers. Of course, molesters don't wear trench coats! You would not leave your child with them if they did.

Knowing who has access to your child should include some basic information:

- Does this person have an unusual interest in your child or children? For example, as a therapist, I see children in my practice on a daily basis. I like kids. At the end of the day, however, I do not have a desire to spend time with other people's children. Ask yourself, "Is this person's interest in my child consistent with his or her role in the child's life?"

- Have there been previous accusations or concerns? I use the word "concerns" because my experience has been "where there is smoke, there is fire." I often meet alleged offenders who report having been accused once, twice, even three times before. They seem puzzled how, on separate occasions, different individuals would make such horrible accusations.

"How many times have you been accused of murder, arson, or theft?" I ask.

"None." The normal reply.

"Why are you being accused of sexual misconduct on several different occasions?" This is a fair question parents should factor into decisions they make about who has access to a child.

The courts have a duty to uphold "innocent until proven guilty." You do not. Listen to that small voice that says, "Something doesn't feel right here."

IGNORANCE IS BLISS, MAN

I present a seminar on child sexual abuse monthly at my office. Attendees are usually dealing with a sexual abuse allegation within their family and are involved with agencies such as the Department of Family Protective Services or the probation department.

Mike and Carla had travelled from out of state to attend the seminar after their five- and seven-year-old daughters accused a (male) friend of the family of sexual abuse. The children had been left in the care of their friend, a recently paroled sex offender, while Mike and Carla spent a long weekend together on Mike's eighteen wheeler, catching up on some "alone time."

I asked, "Why were your children taken from you?"

Mike responded, "Because they say our little girls were sexually abused by our friend. That's ~! @#$. I've known him all my life."

"Why do they say this?" I asked.

Carla responded, "They say it's true because our friend is *supposedly* a sex offender. We know that is not true! He was falsely accused, and he did not abuse our daughters. If he was a sex offender, we wouldn't be leaving our kids with him!"

"What is your goal?" I asked.

Mike answered abruptly, "Our kids back, man! This is *! @#$."

"Let me get this straight," I stated. "You left your little girls with a paroled, registered sex offender over the weekend, alone, because you think he was falsely accused of sexually abusing a child, and now, you think your children are lying?

"You're not getting your kids back, man."

TRUTH IS STRANGER THAN FICTION

A sad but true postscript to Mike and Carla's story: Two years after their children were permanently removed from their care, the couple was again involved with the Department of Family Protective Services. The allegation? Having had a third child, Mike and Carla continued to live with the same paroled, registered sex offender who had cost them their daughters.

CHAPTER TWO: WHO IS AT RISK? SUMMARY

- One out of three girls is estimated to experience sexual abuse before age 18.

- One out of six boys is estimated to experience

sexual abuse before age 18.

- The median age for reported abuse is nine years old.

- More than 20 percent of children are abused before the age of eight years.

- Children are most vulnerable between ages eight and 12.

- The average age for first-time abuse is 9.9 years for boys and 9.6 years for girls.

- Victimization occurs before age eight in more than 20 percent of the cases.

Chapter Three:
Why Survivors Don't Tell

"I couldn't figure out when to ruin my mother's life."
(Jennifer, 16-year-old survivor)

Some startling statistics on the subject of child sexual abuse include the aforementioned one in three girls and one in six boys being sexually abused by their 18th birthday. Another disturbing estimate is that, of all the child sexual abuse that occurs, only 16 percent of the abuse is ever disclosed or reported. [xix]

If the frequency of child sexual abuse is so high, why are there not more disclosures? The answer is victims do not want to tell about their abuse unless they have to. This does not mean the abuse is insignificant or that poor reporting rates reflect that victims do not view their abuse as serious. I believe the opposite is true. The majority of sexual abuse victims never tell because their violation was so profound that they desperately want to shield the people they are closest to from having to experience the matter as well.

NOT UNTIL TODAY . . .

Cloe Madanes, Ph.D., esteemed family therapist, author, and speaker, said, "Sexual abuse is an assault on the soul," suggesting sexual abuse transcends the physical realm and permeates one's core, one's soul, leaving a lasting footprint. [xx]

As a psychotherapist, I thought I understood Madanes's words, when I met a 64-year-old woman. Nana, as she was called, came to me after her eight-year-old granddaughter claimed to have been sexually abused by her mother's boyfriend. After the child made the report, she was removed from the care of her unbelieving, unsupportive mother.

The child had lived with Nana for much of her young life due to her mother's pattern of instability. The two had become very close as Nana had become the primary mother figure in the child's life.

Social Services assumed the child would be placed with Nana. At the initial hearing to remove the child from the abusive home, however, Nana refused to take custody of her granddaughter. Nana simply did not believe the girl was telling the truth about being molested. The child was placed in a shelter, and Nana was referred to me to see if placing the child with Nana could be salvaged.

Nana lived in a small West Texas town much like the one I grew up in. She embodied the West Texas values of honesty and hard work. She had a seasoned toughness about her that I had seen before in people who worked hard all their lives. Years of exposure to the West Texas sun made her appear older than she was. Her hands were rough, fingers crooked with arthritis. She made it clear that seeing a therapist was a waste of time because she wasn't crazy.

I asked Nana about her granddaughter, and softness almost emerged. They were close, she acknowledged. She did not believe, however, the child had been molested. The hardness returned.

"She's lying. I know it," she said.

I replied, "What if you're wrong?"

"I'm not. She's lying." Her voice grew a little harsher.

"I can see you feel strongly about what you believe, but what if you are wrong?"

She responded again even more abruptly, "She's lying. She's lying. I know it."

I wondered if Nana was somehow supporting her daughter's accused boyfriend by not believing the child. "Tell me about the boyfriend. What do you think of him?" I asked.

Nana described the boyfriend as a lazy, controlling thug. She thought her daughter could do better. So much for my theory.

I continued to look for anything that might help me understand Nana's disbelief in her granddaughter. With increasing intensity, she insisted the child was lying.

"You're passionate about what you believe, but could you be passionately wrong?" I finally asked.

"She's lying because she's not acting the way I did when my uncle molested me. I was eight years old, too!" Nana said as she pointed her crooked finger at my face.

Silence.

A single tear moved slowly down Nana's weathered face.

"Did you ever tell anyone about your abuse?" I asked.

She softly replied, "Not until today, you son-of-a @#$%."

Fifty-six years.

Fifty-six years had passed from the time Nana was sexually abused by her uncle to when she sat in a stranger's office—my office—and told of her abuse.

Fifty-six years.

Nana told me she had reported the abuse to her mother only to be dismissed and disbelieved. She described how there were times in her marriage of more than 40 years that she had tried to tell her husband why, at times, she seemed cold and uninterested in the bedroom; why she cringed when he touched her a certain way. She wanted to tell him about the abuse. She could not.

Fifty-six years.

Sexual abuse is an assault on the soul. I understood that now.

WHAT TOOK YOU SO LONG?

Common reasons victims report for not disclosing their abuse include the following:

- Fear

- Embarrassment

- Shame

- Feeling responsible for the abuse

- Protecting the offender

- Protecting other family members

Sixteen-year-old Jennifer started therapy after reporting her biological father had been sexually abusing her over a period of two years.

Jennifer's immediate and extended family members were close. They regularly gathered for lunches and dinners, especially on Sunday afternoons after attending church services. The family had been central members of their church for decades.

Jennifer's accusation against her father sent a shockwave through the family, the church, and the community. Jennifer had developed a reputation for rebellion. Her outcry was met with disbelief by several people, most notably her grandparents and other church members. The prevailing sentiment seemed to be if her father had really sexually abused Jennifer, she would have said something sooner. Not to mention, Jennifer's dad was a long-standing member of the community and the church, with a good reputation.

When I met Jennifer, I knew she had been abandoned by most of the people around her, except for her mother. Her grandparents, her aunts and uncles, her cousins, her church, and the community members seemed eager to dismiss the rebellious teen's accusations as terrible, hurtful lies.

I also knew Jennifer had been close to her grandparents, despite their disapproval of many of her choices. Jennifer was grieving the loss of these relationships.

Because Jennifer's claims were rejected due to the delay in reporting the abuse, I asked her this question, "What took you so long? Why did you wait two years to tell about your abuse?"

Jennifer paused for a moment and then softly said, "I couldn't figure out when to ruin my mother's life. I knew that whenever I told, everything would be different, especially for my mom. That's what took so long."

Jennifer's father eventually admitted having sexually abused both Jennifer and her older sister. Unfortunately, the relationships with those who should have protected, believed, and supported her were forever changed. They failed to recognize that her delayed disclosure was an effort to protect those she cared about, not an indicator of a false allegation.

ZERO. NADA. ZILCH.

When children feel responsible for their abuse, they are less likely to disclose. If they have disclosed, feeling responsible can create a tremendous degree of guilt.

I often ask children in therapy, "How much of the abuse was your fault?" Except on rare occasions, the child indicates feeling responsible for the abuse. Older children may answer in percentages, younger children with phrases or gestures. Usually, the child is carrying feelings of guilt tied to feelings of responsibility. Imagine the courage it takes for the child to disclose being abused when feeling responsible for the abuse.

I had been working with a ten-year-old girl for about three weeks when I asked if she felt responsible for the sexual abuse she had endured at the leisure of her uncle.

In my previous meetings with Shameka, she had never shown emotion. No emotion. No crying. No laughing. No anger. No sadness. Nothing, until I asked that question. It was then that the largest tears I believe I have ever seen appeared in Shameka's deep brown eyes.

"It was my fault," she whispered.
Those eyes.

Mommy, Please Read This

"I could have said no to my uncle, and I didn't."
Those tears.
"I know it was my fault."
Those words.
A handful of Crayons lay on the card table we were sitting at in my playroom.

Any therapist who works with children can tell you the playroom is a magical place. My playroom walls are covered with the traced hands of the children I have treated over the years. Walking into the small room, children are met with little hands everywhere. The message? *"You are not alone."*

When Shameka cried with me, there was only a portion of one wall in the playroom that was not covered with those tiny works of art.

As Shameka insisted the abuse was her fault and her responsibility, I grabbed a Crayon and marked a large zero on the small blank space on the wall.

"That is how much it is your fault. Zero. Not your fault. None. Not your fault."

Silently, Shameka looked at me as if I had lost my mind and then asked if I would get into trouble for writing on the wall.

I laughed.
We laughed.
She cried.
We cried.

A tradition started that day with Shameka. The Crayon zero on the wall of my playroom now has the names of several children who heard for the first time it was not their fault. They get a kick out of getting to write on the wall and not getting into trouble. I get a kick out of helping children put the responsibility where it belongs.

THANKS, MR. TROY

A teenaged male cousin had molested eight-year-old Marcus. When asked how much of the abuse was his responsibility, Marcus reported feeling guilty for the abuse because (1) he should have, could have stopped the abuse, and (2) some of the abuse was physically pleasurable.

I processed the question with Marcus as I always do with children. I clearly explain the abuse was "zero" percent their fault and give examples to reinforce the point. Marcus responded with visible relief to hear he was not to blame.

About an hour after Marcus left my office, I received a call from his mother. "What did you discuss with Marcus today?" she asked. I explained we had visited about feeling responsible for the abuse and inquired if everything was okay. She explained that as she and her son were walking to their car, Marcus turned, look up at my office, and yelled, "Thanks, Mr. Troy!"

It wasn't his fault.

CHAPTER THREE:
WHY SURVIVORS DON'T TELL
SUMMARY

- Most survivors of sexual abuse never disclose their abuse.

- Reasons for not disclosing include fear, shame, guilt, feeling responsible for the abuse, and wanting to protect loved ones.

- Delay in disclosure is normal and does not indicate the abuse was insignificant or did not occur.

Chapter Four: Portrait of a Molester

I am mad because they charged me with Aggravated Sexual Assault of a Child. I did not aggravate anybody!
(50-year-old registered sex offender)

I attended my first group therapy program for sex offenders in 1990. I was a probation officer and was meeting an offender who had been referred to this particular counseling program. I had not met the therapist facilitating the group, and I assumed he would be easy to identify—probably the one in a suit, smoking a pipe, looking like Freud— you know the look.

After locating the building where the group met, I was first surprised at the variety of vehicles in the parking area. There were mostly average cars, a few clunkers, and a few high-priced luxury models. There were a couple of bicycles and a motorcycle or two. There was a large, dirty backpack placed just outside the glass doors of the meeting room. As I soon learned, the placement of the backpack served to allow its owner, a leathered-faced man similar in condition to the pack, to keep watch over his possessions while shielding the rest of us from the unmistakable odor of life on the streets.

I walked into a large room that, ironically, served as a banquet facility for anniversaries, weddings, and reunions. To my surprise, approximately 75 men—sex offenders—were gathering in a large circle as time for the group meeting drew near.

As a new probation officer, I was both curious and disgusted by dealing with sex offenders. To me, a sex offender, a child molester, a baby-raper, a pervert, a pedophile, were all embodied in an image of a dirty, unkempt man in a trench coat.

He was there.

What confused me was how most of the men looked absolutely normal. I wondered, "Am I at the right place? Could there be this many sex offenders in Amarillo, Texas?"

I spotted a clean-cut, middle-aged man taking a seat on the far side of the room. He wore a freshly pressed suit, and while there were others in slacks, dress shirts, etc., this man, this gentleman, wore a tie, carried a notepad, and appeared self-assured as he started to take a chair by trench coat guy.

"He must be the therapist," I thought, as I approached, hand outstretched to introduce myself. Appearing puzzled, the man said, "I'm not the therapist, if that's who you're looking for," as he continued

Portrait of a Molester

to sit down. I looked at trench coat guy as he stood to greet me.

The group was truly a cross sample of men within the community. My mental picture of what a sex offender looks like changed that day. Dozens and dozens of men who looked like banker guy, church guy, and the middle-aged white guy who wants to sell me a car outnumbered trench coat guy. Black guy was there. Brown guy was there. Really, really old guy was there along with a few 17 year olds.

Child molesters seldom fit the image and mold that we have of them in our minds. This works to their advantage. While we focus on trench coats, predators, and stranger danger, the very clever, clean-cut, extraordinarily average child molester is busy being just another guy in the community, with one exception—his sexual interest in children.

By the way, trench coat guy was not the therapist, either. He did, however, point him out to me.

DEMOGRAPHICS OF MOLESTERS

It is generally agreed that no particular profile describes sex offenders. [xxi] In a 2001 landmark study of the demographics of child molesters, Gene Abel, M.D., and Nora Harlow, M.A., demonstrated empirically what I witnessed in the group described above.

Consider the following facts: [xxii]

- Child molesters come from all ethnic, racial, and social groups.

- Child molesters may be heterosexual, homosexual, or bisexual. Interestingly, men who molest boys are reported to be predominantly heterosexual (80 percent).

- Child molesters may be male or female. While the majority of known offenders are male (90 percent), the estimates of female offenders are likely underestimated.

Female offenders are often viewed differently from their male counterparts. For example, in a 1995 case, a 34-year-old woman was arrested and indicted for having sex with five 12-year-old boys. The woman was placed on five separate probation cases. I think it would be very unlikely that a male offender under the same circumstances would have received probation.

The aforementioned study conducted by the U.S. Department of Justice found that female offenders, while rare in comparison to their male counterparts, were most common in assaults against victims younger than age six.

Interestingly, society seems to view female offenders and their victims differently from male offenders and their victims. Some researchers sug-

Portrait of a Molester

gest this is related to our inherent need to protect little girls from abuse and easily seeing them as victims. With boys, on the other hand, sexual contact with a woman is often not seen as abuse at all, rather "the kid earning his stripes." This could not be further from the truth.

Infamous female offenders such as Mary Kay Letourneau, the Washington teacher who became pregnant by her 13-year-old student, illustrate the varying ways we view such abuse. Now married, the convicted sex offender and her victim/husband have reportedly hosted several "Hot for Teacher Night" promotions at a Seattle nightclub. [xxiii] Ask yourself, if Letourneau were a man and the victim a girl, would a "Hot for Teacher" promotion be considered acceptable?

The fact is, when an offender, female or male, takes advantage of a child, there is always an effect. Letourneau's victim, for example, had his life changed by her abuse. Even had she not become pregnant with the teen's baby, she introduced him to a life-changing, thought-changing, person-changing experience called "sex."

BUT HE'S SO NICE . . .

Consider this case. Paul was a good guy. He regularly volunteered to help with the children's ministry in his church. He had previously been involved with Kid's Incorporated, Big Brothers/Big Sisters, a community soccer league for children, and a couple of faith-based service organizations designed to assist children. Heterosexual, never married, mid-30s, handsome, educated, well spoken, and unselfish with his time when it came to helping others, especially children—this described Paul.

Another description of Paul was also quietly voiced from time to time. Over the course of 12 years, Paul had been asked to leave one organization after another due to concerns expressed by parents. Although no formal accusations had been made, parents notified the leadership of the organizations that something about how Paul interacted with the children made their parents uncomfortable. In response, the organizations politely asked Paul to move on, so as not to embarrass anyone. No reports to law enforcement were ever made.

In 2006, Paul pled guilty to Indecency with a Child for molesting children in his care in a children's ministry. He has since acknowledged having struggled with masturbatory fantasies of children most of his adult life and recently admitted having as many as 50 victims.

Parents' concerns about Paul were correct. The failure of several organizations to act on these concerns allowed Paul to continue his abusive behavior.

Listen to your feelings when it comes to how others interact with your children.

I created a presentation for seminars that includes admitted molesters describing their offenses in an audio recording. While hearing the offender, the audience sees a description of the offender's age and occupation projected onscreen. The piece includes a retired service officer, plumber, policeman, lesbian, men and women, old, young, poor, and extremely wealthy. It is truly a cross-section of the offending population in my hometown.

Who audiences do not hear from are strangers. All the molesters in the project had known their victims before the offense and, with few exceptions, were either friends of the victim's family or family members themselves.

HAVE TOOLS. WILL TRAVEL.

I invited a sex offender to speak to a support group I met with each month. The meeting was to begin at 6:00 p.m., and people began to assemble in the meeting room next to my office. Jerry, the offender, arrived and asked if he could go ahead into the room. I had taken a last-minute telephone call so it was just after six when I walked into the meeting. Jerry and eight or so women were discussing his work as a handyman. I noticed that each lady held in her possession one of Jerry's business cards. The conversation was friendly. The women were interested in hearing from this charming, talented, handsome fellow, who was, like them, there to learn about sexual abuse. Probably there to see and hear firsthand from one of "them."

I took my seat as a Jerry continued describing his various skills while arranging a date to provide an estimate for one of the ladies.

"Tonight, as you know," I said, "we will be hearing from an admitted child molester about how he chose potential victims and how he gained their trust. Jerry, thank you for agreeing to share your story with our group."

I wish I knew how to write the sound of a car coming to a screeching stop or the sound of an LP record being stopped suddenly with the record player needle dragged across the song because that is what the moment was like.

Jerry took it from there.

"Thank you, Troy. Hello, I am Jerry, and I am a registered sex offender. I sexually abused my . . ."

Before Jerry could finish his introduction, the woman who had been arranging for an estimate in her home—by Jerry the handyman—had gathered enough composure to announce, "Holy! @#$! You're the sex offender? You were in here visiting with us, handing out your cards, being, being, being *(this is not a typo. She really did repeat the word)* nice!"

Nobody spoke as Jerry's torn business card fell to the floor and the woman walked out of the meeting, betrayed by Jerry the handyman.

CHAPTER FOUR: PORTRAIT OF A MOLESTER SUMMARY

- The average sexual abuser is just that, incredibly average.

- Most child sex abusers are known and trusted adults in the child's life.

- There is no profile of child sex offenders.

- Males make up the majority of molesters; however, females also molest children.

Chapter Five:
How Molesters Operate

"If you don't want to spend time with your kid, I will."
(26-year-old registered sex offender)

Want to rob a bank? Talk to a successful bank robber. I ask child molesters this simple question: "What is the most effective way to set up a potential victim?" Overwhelmingly, the response has been:

- Listen to the child.

- Spend time with the child.

- Pick the least assertive child.

Consider these comments made by molesters:

I find common ground with the child. I want to find an activity or subject that is interesting to them, that allows them to relax and open up. From there, other subjects and activities can be approached. I want to make them and their interests the priority.

Befriend them. Be nice to them. Give them special benefits. Most of all, I would pay attention to them, find common ground, and gain their trust.

I want to gain their trust. I would make a game out of it, tell them it is o.k., and be sure to give them special attention.

I want to spend time alone with the child. I gain their trust by giving them my attention. I am the person they can tell anything.

You need to keep a closer eye on your children, their behavior, and the people they are hanging out with. Because if you are not, you can bet I am. That is what I do. <u>I watch and become what you are not</u>. If you do not listen, I will. If you are overbearing, then I am not. If you do not show appreciation, I will. If you do not have time, I do.

I gain their trust by spending time with them and making it really about them. If you don't want to spend time with your kid, I will.

These offenders are answering the question parents need to ask, "How is a person I know and trust able to sexually abuse a child and nobody seems to notice?"

The answer is called "grooming."

Grooming is what sex offenders do to gain the trust of, first, the child's caregivers and, second, the targeted child. Sex offenders groom their target victims to pursue sexual activity with the child and to encourage secrecy.

Numerous researchers have found that 80 percent of sex offenders use grooming as their primary method to facilitate the abuse. [xxiv] Only 10 percent are thought to use threats of force, and 10 percent use actual force to execute the abuse. The fact is, most offenders do not use threats or force because they do not have to. If they have successfully groomed the victim and the victim's family, neither is necessary.

ANGEL SENT FROM HEAVEN

In 2004, I was called as an expert witness in a sexual abuse trial involving a 34-year-old man accused of repeatedly molesting twin, teenaged boys he had met while they lived in a residential placement. The boys were voluntarily placed in the residential setting for one year by their mother who was experiencing serious health and financial difficulties. It was in the placement the boys met Jones, a case manager within the agency.

After a year, the boys returned to their mother's care. While Mom's condition had improved, life for the family continued to be marked by financial instability and simply having less than others.

Mommy, Please Read This

Shortly after the boys' return home, Jones showed up at the boys' home, introduced himself to the twins' mother as a caseworker with the placement agency, and reintroduced himself to the boys. They remembered him from the placement, having had occasional contact with him. Jones had not abused the boys during their placement.

Jones offered to provide any assistance he could to the family, suggesting his help was part of his job, but also because he had noticed the boys were desperately in need of an appropriate male role model—a big brother of sorts.

Jones began making regular contact with the mother to check on the boys and to see if they needed anything. Although guarded toward him at first, Mother eventually began accepting Jones's offers to help.

On one occasion, the washing machine was broken, and the dirty clothes were piling up. Jones remarked he had a friend with rental properties who would let him have a washer for little or no money. That afternoon, Mother graciously accepted the appliance and began washing what clothes the boys had.

Teenagers of course want cool stuff. Cool stuff costs money. This family had neither. Jones, recognizing an opportunity to build the relationship, began providing gifts, cool gifts, to the boys. Now, they, too, had the Starter jackets their classmates wore. Now, they too, had the Air Jordans they thought they could never afford. Now, in a sense, they had a father figure who seemed to always do the right thing. They were

How Molesters Operate

hooked.

In court, Mother described believing Jones was an angel sent to help her family during some of their most difficult times. Because of this, when Jones asked to take the twins on a day trip out of town to see an air show, she agreed, as the boys enthusiastically insisted.

A few weeks later, Jones asked for the boys to attend another air show; this one, however, was too far away for a day trip. "O.K. to spend the night and let the boys swim at the hotel? They had such a great time at the last show," he remarked.

With numerous examples of Jones's generosity, no inappropriate behavior toward the boys, and the twins enthusiastically enjoying their relationship with the dad they never had but had always wanted, Mother again allowed the boys to go. After all, this angel was so good for the boys. They had never seemed happier.

The evening of the air show (after swimming in the hotel pool and after allowing the boys to drink the alcohol he had brought along), Jones began molesting the twins. He explained to them that one way for them to show their love and appreciation for all that he had done for them and their mother would be to be sexual with him. After all, this is one way that fathers and sons—real fathers and sons—show love for each other.

The abuse continued for three years.

Interestingly, the defense and prosecution of this case both seemed to be centered on grooming. The prosecutors argued Jones had spent months grooming the boys and their mother for the abuse. The defense argued that Jones, after giving so much of himself, was being falsely accused by ungrateful adolescents who constantly wanted more and more from him.

Jones never made threats or used force to facilitate the abuse of these children. He was never romantically interested in their mother. He was viewed as "an angel sent from Heaven" because he *successfully groomed the family system.*

It is common for victims to describe their abusers as one of their closest, most adored relationships. This occurs because, while the offender's motive for grooming is deviant, the relationship that results can be very rewarding to the child. This profound violation of trust creates enormous internal conflict for the child.

A couple of years after Jones was found guilty and sentenced to 45 years in prison, one of the twins came to see me. The awkward teen I had last seen in a courtroom was now a handsome, strong young man. As we discussed his adjustment, he tearfully commented that he had genuinely loved Jones as the father he always wanted. His struggle now was trying to make sense of the competing emotions of love and hate for his abuser.

We would like to have a way to identify child molesters. Unfortunately, no profile, psychological assessment, psychosexual assessment, or battery of tests is able to identify child molesters *before* they molest.

I have met many, many people who were shocked to learn a particular person had molested a child. This seems to be related to the idea that we tend to have friendships with persons we see as being similar to us. If it turns out our trusted friend, spouse, or relative is a child molester, it is hard to believe, in part, because we see that person as being similar to us. That person is not. Child molesters are skilled masters at the art of deception. They can groom the most careful and suspicious caregivers. That is what sets child molesters apart.

It would be easier if they all wore trench coats.

CLOSE TO HOME

Kanakuk is a faith-based summer camp in Missouri that has served children for decades. In 2009, the ministry was rocked by allegations of sexual abuse by Peter Newman, a respected camp director that had been with Kanakuk for over ten years.

Interestingly, we were in the process of enrolling my nine-year-old son in Kanakuk when news of the sexual abuse scandal broke. We have several friends whose children have attended the camp, one who had actually been a guest in Newman's home. Needless to say, they were shocked by the allegations. Expressions of disbelief, anger, disappointment, and fear were core ingredients of the conversations taking place. Some families chose to return to Kanakuk. Some did not.

In June 2010, I was in Branson, Missouri dropping off my son at the camp. That same week Peter Newman was sentenced to two life sentences plus 30 years for abusing boys in his care. A local newspaper reported the following: "Pete worked at a slow pace, by 'hanging out' with them, doing sleepovers, meeting their parents and thereby, gaining their trust. He would further his friendship by taking the kids on vacation, retreats, send letters, e-mails, phone calls, etc., and then continued by inviting them over for group Bible studies and even furthered his 'friendship' by having one-on-one Bible sessions in his hot tub at his residence."

What happened at Kanakuk is a classic example of how molesters operate. Unfortunately, the result of one person's behavior had a negative impact on countless numbers of people and the ministry itself.

As my wife and I discussed our decision to allow our son to attend Kanakuk, I had to remind myself of all the information I am asking others to consider. Even armed with the facts, I found myself anxious about the "what if's" of trusting my child in someone else's care. While Newman will never know it, his abusive behavior affected a family in Texas, my family, and many, many others.

Such is abuse.

CHAPTER FIVE:
HOW MOLESTERS OPERATE
SUMMARY

- Eighty percent of child sexual abuse involves "grooming."

- Ten percent involves threats of force.

- Ten percent involves actual force.

- Offenders report their most effective strategy for setting up a child for abuse is to listen to the child and be attentive to the child's needs.

Chapter Six:
Responding Appropriately To Child Sexual Abuse

"The sexual abuse sucked. Not being believed hurt."
(25-year-old survivor)

Sexual abuse is a contradiction of so many things. Tonight, I quietly observed a 43-year-old mother sob—not cry—sob for her molested child. She wept for the loss her family had suffered over the past year after her husband admitted sexually abusing their 11-year-old daughter.

"Anger, rage, hate, darkness, destroy, kill, evil. That's what I feel," she said.

In a strange twist of events, while she sat sobbing in my office, torn with hurt, anger, hate, rage, and darkness, an admitted sex offender sat in the adjacent office laughing loudly in conversation with his therapist.

Sobbing.
Laughing.
Crying.
Making small talk.
Raging.
Manipulating.

The tragedy played out in front of me. A victim's heartbroken mother sat in my office.

A perpetrator sat in the office next door. Both were hurting, but in very different ways.

If the numbers of children who will experience sexual abuse before their 18th birthday are correct, there is, unfortunately, a great likelihood that a child you know has been, or will be, sexually abused.

BELIEVE

Victims of sexual abuse are re-traumatized each time they risk telling their story and are not believed.

Your first and most important task is to BELIEVE your child. If you do not believe your child is telling the truth, two things will likely occur. First, your child may recant (take back) the allegation. Second, you have taught your child that the adults who are supposed to protect him or her cannot be trusted. The latter creates a tear in the parent-child relationship that never heals completely.

LISTEN

Imagine sitting at the dinner table with your children. In the background, you hear a television news story about a child molester. Dad says, "If that ever happened to my child, I would kill that S.O.B." Here's the catch. The child at the table is being abused and just heard Dad threaten to kill the abuser—a close friend of the family.

Our children are listening.

Their ability to approach us with important problems is affected by how we react before the abuse occurs.

I MISS MY DAD

The difference between hearing and listening is, when we hear someone, we find ourselves thinking about how we will respond, what we will say. When we listen, our response takes a back seat to validating the person's story. The art of listening can never be overstated.

I was in over my head. Having recently completed graduate school, I was fortunate to be working in a group practice owned by a child psychologist with decades of experience. I was seeing children in a small outlying town, most of whom were involved with social services. Four-year-old Carlos was one of these children.

Carlos became selectively mute after his father committed suicide. I was seeing Carlos in weekly play

Mommy, Please Read This

therapy, reporting on the child's adjustment to my employer and the other therapists in the practice in a weekly staff meeting. I was intrigued by the case and wanted to somehow help Carlos with his trauma. I also wanted to impress my employer and those in the practice. Week after week, I updated the group with a lengthy synopsis of the therapy. Carlos' condition had not improved.

After presenting the case for the third week in a row, my psychologist employer asked to see me after the meeting. "This child," he said, "desperately needs his therapist to be listening to him—emotionally, physically, spiritually—listening. If you are planning your next presentation to us when you are with him, you are not doing your job, and you are letting Carlos down."

Ouch.

Admonished and embarrassed, I committed myself to take his words to heart. My sessions with Carlos continued as I focused my attention on the child without allowing myself to be distracted by thoughts of how I was doing. It wasn't about me.

Weeks later, Carlos remained selectively mute, but was becoming more engaged in telling his story through play. Something was changing.

Having completed yet another session with Carlos, I walked to my desk, took my seat, and prepared to make a brief note in his chart. Silently, the dark-haired boy appeared next to me and then quickly climbed onto the desk, sitting on my chart. We faced each other in silence.

"Mr. Troy?" he quietly spoke. "I miss my dad."

Carlos slid off the desk to leave as I noted the lump in my throat and the tremendous value of what I had just heard and learned.

SARA

Sara's trial ended yesterday. It was an awful reminder of what children suffer at the hands of their abusers. In this case, the offender was Sara's father, and the abuse went on for months. He had confessed to most of the horrific acts against his daughter. I think he insisted on going to a jury trial, even though he knew he would be sentenced to prison, for one last opportunity to molest Sara, at least in his mind, one last chance to relive the abuse, one last chance to hurt.

"When he was making me do that, I couldn't breathe. He felt my tears running down my face, and he still didn't stop," Sara softly told the misty-eyed jurors as she was made to describe her abuse in front of the monster who had betrayed her. By the end of the trial, she was exhausted.

Sara met me at my office the day after her father was sentenced to 435 years in prison. She quietly sat in a large leather chair, staring sadly at the floor. Accompanying me to the office was Garvin, my normally energetic Labradoodle (especially around children). Not today.

As if he knew Sara needed calm. As if he knew Sara craved peace. As if he knew Sarah, Garvin slowly approached her, laying his head in her lap, showing me what listening looks like.

HOW TO TALK TO A CHILD ABOUT SEXUAL ABUSE [xxv]

Responding appropriately to child sexual abuse requires a before-and-after plan. Long before a family is touched by an accusation, parents need to be calm when discussing the issue. After an allegation arises, calm, confident listening is the key. I want the message from parents to be, "Now that I know, I am strong, and I will protect you."

If a child you know hints, even in a vague way, that abuse has occurred, listen to him or her. Stay calm. Tell your child that you would like to help him or her. Children frequently report abuse a little at a time to see how you will react and determine your trustworthiness.

The Bridge Children's Advocacy Center provides the following suggestions for talking to a child about sexual abuse:

- Be patient, calm, and supportive. If a child comes to you, sit down and calmly say, "Tell me about what happened."

- If you notice that a child is acting out, or asks questions that seem advanced, calmly ask him or her,

Responding Appropriately to Child Abuse

"Where did you hear or learn that?"

- Tell the child that you believe him or her. Assure the child that he or she did the right thing in telling.

- Find out how the child feels physically. Ask if he or she is hurting anywhere.

- Watch both your verbal and nonverbal language. Be careful of scaring the child by exhibiting strong emotions, such as anger.

- Do not question the child extensively or make the child tell more than one person.

- Don't introduce or suggest names either of persons or of body parts. Use the child's terminology. Introducing new words can often cause confusion. Allow the child to tell what happened in his or her words.

- Do not take the law into your own hands and confront the perpetrator or make the child confront the perpetrator. Allow the investigators to determine the steps to be taken.

- Be supportive of the child. Tell the child that he or she is very brave for speaking up and telling someone.

- Make a report. Report it IMMEDIATELY to your local law enforcement agency or child welfare department.

- Resist the urge to "protect the child" by not reporting the incident.

Many parents rightly question if the trauma of reporting will be as hurtful to the victim as the abuse itself. They fear their children being interviewed by strangers, undergoing embarrassing and invasive examinations, and being called a liar. They worry that, ultimately, the system will do little or nothing to the molester, even if found guilty. In short, they ask if reporting the abuse is worth the pain that may come with telling.

I have seen the pain of making a report play out in families and communities many times. I have also interviewed those who were rewarded when the report was not made. Molesters frequently report having experienced previous allegations that were never officially reported. Michael, an admitted molester, recently said, "I got braver when I knew no report would be made simply because I insisted it was not true. I knew then I had the upper hand." While not reporting may allow us to avoid obviously frightening experiences, ultimately failing to report child abuse allows molesters to continue their abuse. And they will.

CHAPTER SIX: RESPONDING APPROPRIATELY TO CHILD SEXUAL ABUSE SUMMARY

- Remain calm when discussing sexual abuse with children.

- Believe your child.

- Listen to the child and be supportive.

- Report the abuse allegation immediately.

Chapter Seven:

Preventing Child Sexual Abuse

My colleague, Gaye Bennett, wrote an op-ed piece for a local newspaper regarding zoning restrictions and registered offenders. A newer housing development had recently advertised the area as being free of sexual offenders by restricting known offenders from buying or leasing homes in the area. Ms. Bennett wrote the following:

> *I agree with a developer's right to prohibit registered sex offenders from living in his neighborhood because, as a private business entity, he should be allowed to make business decisions based on his own convictions. If banning this group of people were to save even one potential victim, it would be worth it.*

However, I believe this restriction only can give the illusion of safety to families living in this neighborhood. While it is a noble effort to curb the ever-growing epidemic of sexual abuse (and, I must admit, a great marketing tool), there is little evidence that banning registered sex offenders will decrease the incidence of abuse.

There have been similar bans implemented; however, the logic behind them often is based on myth:

It is a myth that most sex offenders are strangers to their victims. Ninety percent of sex crimes are perpetrated by someone the victim knows, not a stranger. Live-in partners and acquaintances of the family are more likely to cross the line sexually than a stranger down the street. In these instances, the child is less safe in his own home than he is out riding his bike in a neighborhood where registered sex offenders live.

It is a myth that all registered sex offenders will commit another sex crime. While most sex offenders in Texas are required to register in the same way, not all sex crimes are created equal. I agree with the November 29 Globe-News editorial, "There goes the neighborhood," that there is a wide spectrum of sex offenders who range from low to high risk, yet they all are given the same label and demonized along with the most dangerous of sexual predators.

Many offenders will learn a hard lesson from treatment and the legal system. They will put proper boundaries on their behavior and go on to become productive citizens in our community.

If a registered sex offender is living in your community, it is likely he is currently under supervision or allowed freedom based on completion of treatment and his legal sentence. That offender needs the opportunity to better himself, to be part of a family, part of a work force and part of a community. It is estimated that after treatment, fewer than 10 percent of sex offenders will commit another sex crime.

Even with data from research, can we yet predict anyone's individual behavior? Absolutely not! The banning policy may prevent the registered sex offender from living in this housing addition, but there is no way to shut out the untreated sex abuser who is contemplating a destructive choice.

There is no way to shut out the drug user who might introduce your child to illegal drugs. There is no way to shut out the thief or the depressed teen who might open fire on the neighbors.

There is no such thing as a completely safe neighborhood, because neighborhoods are made up of people. And people sometimes make destructive choices.

And here's an interesting thought: Is it possible that the illusion of safety might cause people

> *to let down their guard and be less aware of impending risk? Could cases of sexual abuse actually increase?* [xxvi]

All responsible parents want their children to be safe from sexual exploitation. Unfortunately, our focus on stranger danger, coupled with an irrational fear of registered sex offenders, has distracted parents from the real risk our families face.

HEY, MISTER

A child's idea of who is a stranger is different from yours and mine.

Some children never meet a stranger. My nine year old son is like that. He has the unique ability and confidence to carry on a conversation with practically anyone. For example, he recently provided free and unsolicited advice to an unknown golfer some 60 years his senior on the practice green. I asked him why he thought it okay to approach the stranger. He responded, "Well, Dad, somebody had to tell him why he was missing all those putts."

Many children view a stranger as a person they have not interacted with.

In the fall of each year, my son's elementary school has a carnival. Games for the children are erected on the parking lot of the school, food is prepared, prizes are awarded, and children from kindergarten to fifth grade drag parents from one exciting exercise to another.

As I stood with my first grader in line for the ring-toss, an older boy (I soon learned he was a fourth grader) asked, "Hey, Mister. Are you in line for this game?"

"Yes," I replied.

"Hey, Mister," he continued. "Let me cut in front of you. You're too old to be in line for this game."

"Old? I'm not old. I'm in the fourth grade," I responded.

The boy shot back, "You're not in the fourth grade. I'm in the fourth grade, and I don't know you. Let me cut in front of you."

The child's friend, seeing and hearing our conversation, warned the boy that he should not be talking to a stranger (me).

"He's not a stranger. He's in the fourth grade with me, dummy!"

ME, TOO

Often, when I meet a young client for the first time at my office, the child's parent remarks, "He or she is very shy and may not agree to talk with you." I have handled this situation the same way for years.

> Me: "Hi, I'm Troy. What's your name?"
> Child: "Billy."

Me: "How old are you?"
Child: "Six."
Me: "Me too."
Child "You're not six!"
Me: "Oh you caught me. Would you like me to show you around the office? I have a playroom."

Parents are usually surprised at how quickly their child opens up to me, the stranger. Here is what is unsettling. Child molesters are better at establishing rapport with children than most of us. Simply telling your child to not talk to strangers is not enough to keep your child safe.

SUGGESTIONS FOR PREVENTION

As one can see, teaching our children about stranger danger is not enough to protect them from sexual abuse. The following are suggestions for preventing sexual abuse in your family:

Discuss what "private parts" mean with your children.

I explain this as areas that are covered by your swimsuit. Children should be taught that they have the right to determine who may touch them in this area.

Explain that people in your child's life have a specific role or function.

For example, the soccer coach teaches how to kick the ball, the piano instructor teaches music, and the Sunday school teacher provides religious instruction. None of these jobs will EVER include sexual touch. In fact, there are likely only two or three people in the entire world—parent, doctor, approved caregiver—who would EVER need to interact with the child in a way that would include touching or exposing private areas (bathing, hygiene, etc.).

Do not put teenaged boys in situations where they will have to deal with a child's bathing/bathroom needs.

Recent studies estimate that teenaged males commit half of the sexual abuse perpetrated against young children. I recently asked several juvenile sex offenders to provide an overview of "the ingredients" of their sexual offense(s). These young offenders offered the following recipe:

> 1 part curiosity
> 1 part pornography
> 1 part access to a younger child
> 1 part inadequate supervision

The day before I left to speak at a conference in Dallas, a local minister met with me to obtain information about dealing with sexual abuse within the Church. It seems the small, understaffed organization, had made a regular practice of allowing the Youth to supervise children too young to attend the regular service. Consequently, one of the young men was accused of inappropriately touching a child in his care. We discussed the situation and the pastor asked how I believe he should proceed.

"You should report the incident to the authorities, if you have not already, and you should contact your attorney and insurance carrier." I said.

"Oh, no. We have discussed the matter within the church and prefer to handle it within the organization. Is there anything else we should do at this point?"

"You must report the matter the authorities, that's the law. You should also inform your insurance carrier and attorney of the situation in case the church is sued. Why are you reluctant to do these things?" I asked.

The pastor replied, "We just don't want to make this any more difficult than it has to be" and thanked me for my time.

While I was away, a lawsuit brought against a church for failing to protect against sexual abuse by appropriately screening caregivers was announced in the media. When I returned, I had a message from the pastor with this question, "Can you recommend an attorney?"

Talk to your children about strangers, but keep it in perspective.

Remember, a child is more likely to be struck by lightning than abducted and abused by a stranger.

Model and encourage assertiveness.

Offenders tell us they are looking for the least assertive child as their potential victim. Consider how we teach subtle lessons to our children that they are not to tell adults "no." The family reunion, for example, where we push our children into the arms and laps of virtual strangers to avoid appearing impolite, reinforces that children cannot say "no" to adults. Offenders report seeking out the less assertive child as a potential victim, hoping that the quieter child will be less likely to report the abuse. Teaching and modeling assertiveness make children less of a target and more likely to speak up if abused.

SEVEN STEPS TO PROTECTING OUR CHILDREN: [xxvii]

Darkness to Light offers the following "Seven Steps to Protecting Our Children:"

Step 1: Learn the Facts

Realities, not trust, should influence your decisions regarding your child.

I recently testified in a trial where the defense put on several life-long friends of the defendant. Each testified about having absolutely no reservations about the accused (an admitted molester) being around children, even their own.

This degree of naive trust is dangerous and places children at risk of being abused.

Step 2: Minimize Opportunity

If you eliminate or reduce one-adult/one-child situations, you will dramatically lower the risk of sexual abuse for your child.

This step encourages accountability and, I believe, will result in the decrease of both true and false allegations of child sex abuse (although current rates of false outcries are extremely low). In fact, one study found less than two percent of abuse reports made by children and six percent of those made by adults were judged false, suggesting that false allegations are rare. In one study, all but two children who revoked claims of abuse later disclosed new incidents of abuse.

Step 3: Talk about It

Children often keep abuse a secret, but talking openly about it can break down barriers.

I suggest parents teach children the proper names for private parts—penis, vagina, breasts, and buttocks. Listen for any changes in terms used to describe the private parts and follow up by asking, "Where did you hear that word?"

Step 4: Stay Alert

Don't expect obvious signs when a child is being sexually abused.

Researchers report that one third of survivors have no observable symptoms. Don't make the mistake of thinking the abuse must not have occurred simply because the survivor appears to be doing well.

Step 5: Make a Plan

Learn where to go, who to call, and how to react.

Ask yourself, "Whom would I call? Where would I go to get the information and help my child would need?"

Step 6: Act on Suspicions

The future well being of a child is at stake.

Most states provide the opportunity to report suspicions of child abuse to the authorities. If you do not act on your concerns, a child may continue to be abused.

Step 7: Get Involved

Volunteer and/or financially support organizations that fight the tragedy of child sexual abuse.

Find out about your area's Child Advocacy Centers, Department of Child and Family Services, or shelters that serve families dealing with abuse. Numerous opportunities to donate resources and time are likely available. Organizations such as Generation FIVE, Stop It Now!, and Darkness to Light are national movements that I hope you will consider supporting. Locally, there are usually Child Advocacy Centers in need of our time and resources.

WARNING SIGNS TO WATCH FOR:

Ask yourself if you know an adult or an older child who does the following:

- Refuses to let a child or teenager set any of his or her own limits?

Molesters are often very controlling of children in their care.

- Insists on hugging, touching, kissing, tickling, wrestling with, or holding a child even when the child does not want affection?

Molesters "accidently" touch the child's private areas during play, often dismissed as "horseplay," to measure how much sexual touch the child will tolerate.

- Is overly interested in the sexuality of a particular child or teen?

Frequent inquiries about the child's sexual development and sexual relationships are often seen with incest offenders.

- Manages to get time alone or insists on uninterrupted time alone with a child?

Molesters seek out "special time" with the potential victim, exploiting the child's natural desire for attention.

- Spends most of his or her spare time with children and has little interest in spending time with people his or her own age?

Ask yourself if the interest in the child appears to be outside the scope of the relationship.

- Regularly offers to babysit many different children for free or takes children on overnight outings alone?

I have often heard, "I just like spending time with kids." Normal adult men do not want to babysit your kids for free.

- Buys children expensive gifts or gives them money for no apparent reason?

This is a classic grooming technique. Always ask if your child has something you did not provide for him or her.

- Offers alcohol or drugs to teenagers or children when other adults are not around?

Providing alcohol and drugs to the child elevates the child to adult status and acts as a disinhibitor.

- Frequently walks in on children/teens in the bathroom?

Often made to appear an accident. This is a form of voyeurism and yet another opportunity for the molester to approach the subject of sex.

- Allows children or teens to consistently get away with inappropriate behaviors?

This is another way to gain the child's trust while elevating him or her to adult status.

- Often has a "special" child friend, maybe a different one from year to year?

Again, normal adults do not have "special friends" who are children, particularly within a relationship that does not involve the child's parent/guardian or an appropriately screened organization such as Big Brothers/Big Sisters.

- Does not have any close adult friends?

Molesters often struggle maintaining close relationships with adults due to fear of being found out and/or rejected.

- Talks again and again about the sexual activities of children or teens?

I had a patient who regularly quizzed his teenaged stepdaughter about her sexual development and activity. He also made sexual comments about the child to his male friends, some of whom later testified against him at his trial.

- Encourages secrets with a child?

Molesters encourage secrecy. Teach your child the difference between secrets and surprises.

- Discusses sexual matters with children?

Molesters seek out opportunities to discuss sexual matters with children, failing to recognize the obvious inappropriateness of doing so.

CHAPTER SEVEN: PREVENTING CHILD SEXUAL ABUSE SUMMARY

- Get the facts about what to look for in a possible abuser.

- Teach ASSERTIVENESS to your children.

Mommy, Please Read This

- Spend time with your children.
- Listen to your children.
- Talk with your children about the various "jobs" that people have in their lives.

Conclusion
About the Author
Resources
Endnotes

Conclusion

Sexual abuse of children has reached epidemic proportions in the United States. Fully one third of girls and one sixth of boys will be sexually abused before their 18th birthday. These staggering figures must not be ignored.

The goal of this book was to provide you with accurate, easily understood information on child sexual abuse. Unchallenged, the many myths that exist about child sexual abuse place children at greater risk of being abused. Your effort to get the facts is the first critical step to helping prevent abuse.

Knowing, for example, that 90 percent of child sexual abuse is perpetrated by a trusted friend or family member is critical. Knowing how offenders operate and what characteristics offenders seek out in potential victims is critical. Knowing how to help a child who has been abused is critical.

Child molesters are skilled at developing relationships with potential victims, and exploiting the child's natural desire for unconditional love. Offenders have taught me that their greatest asset is their ability to listen, really listen, to the children they intend to molest. What does that say about what we need to do?

One last thought—while researchers report an epidemic of abuse taking place around us, there are also countless heroes among us. You and I have the power to start an epidemic of safety within our families and communities. I believe, armed with the correct information, heroes will emerge, children are protected, and healing begins.

About the Author

Troy D. Timmons, M.Ed., L.P.C., is a Licensed Professional Counselor and Licensed Sex Offender Treatment Provider in private practice in Amarillo, Texas. He provides expert testimony in child abuse cases and speaks at seminars and conferences on child abuse.

For comments about this book, speaking engagements and conference information, write, email or call:

Troy D. Timmons, M.Ed., L.P.C.
7460 Golden Pond Place, Suite 100
Amarillo, Texas 79121 Tel: 806.379.8282
Email: Timmons@sbcglobal.net
Website: www.troytimmons.com

Resources

FOR GENERAL QUESTIONS ABOUT SEXUAL ABUSE OF CHILDREN:

Stop It Now!
351 Pleasant St., Suite 319, Northampton, MA 01060
Office: (413) 587-3500
Helpline: 1.888.PREVENT (1.888.773.8368)
Email: info@stopitnow.org
Website: www.stopitnow.org

Child Welfare Information Gateway Children's Bureau/ACYF.
1250 Maryland Avenue, SW, Eighth Floor, Washington, DC 20024
Office: 703.385.7565 or 800.394.3366
Website: www.childwelfare.gov

A resource and clearinghouse that collects, stores, organizes, and disseminates information on all aspects of child maltreatment

Prevent Child Abuse America (PCAA).
200 South Michigan Ave., 17th Floor
Chicago, IL 60604-2404
Office: (312) 663-3520 Fax: (312) 939-8962
Website: www.preventchildabuse.org

A volunteer-based organization committed to preventing child abuse in all its forms through research, public education, programs, and advocacy. Write for a catalogue of publications.

IF YOU HAVE QUESTIONS ABOUT CRISIS INTERVENTION, TREATMENT, OR REPORTING:

Child Help USA National Child Abuse Hotline.
1-800-4-A-CHILD (1-800-422-4453)
Website: www.childhelpusa.org

The organization provides a broad continuum of programs that directly serve abused children and their families. Adults and children can request local telephone numbers to report cases of abuse or access crisis intervention, information, literature, and referrals to thousands of emergency, social service, and support resources. All calls are anonymous and confidential.

National Center for Missing and Exploited Children (NCMEC).
Charles B. Wang International Children Building
699 Prince Street, Alexandria, VA 22314-3175

Resources

Office: (703) 274-3900 Fax: (703) 274-2220
Website: www.ncmec.org

A clearinghouse for information about the prevention of child victimization. NCMEC's website offers a wealth of information about child protection.

The CyberTipline.
1-800-THE-LOST (1-800-843-5678)

A toll-free line to report any information pertaining to the sexual exploitation of children on the web or any industry that makes use of child pornography (report online at www.cybertipline.com).

CMHS Mental Health Services Locator.
Office: 1-800-789-2647 M-F 8:30 AM to 12:00 AM EST.
Website: www.mentalhealth.samhsa.gov/databases

This locator provides you with comprehensive information about mental health services and resources and is useful for professionals, consumers, and their families, and the public. You can access this information in several ways by selecting a state or U.S. territory from the map or drop-down menu.

National Center for Victims of Crime (NCVC).
2000 M Street N.W., Suite 480, Washington, DC 20036
Office: (202) 467-8700 Fax. (202) 467-8701
Toll-free: 1-800-FYI-CALL (1-800-394-2255)

TDD: 1-800-211-7996
Email: webmaster@ncvc.org or gethelp@ncvc.org
Website: www.ncvc.org

An information and referral center for victims. Through a database of more than 30,000 organizations, NCVC refers callers to critical services, including crisis intervention, research information, assistance with the criminal justice process, counseling, support groups, and referrals to local attorneys in victim-related cases.

The National Children's Advocacy Center (NCAC).
200 Westside Square, Suite 700, Huntsville, AL 35801
Office: (256) 533-0531 Fax: (256) 534-6883
Website: www.nationalcac.org

A nonprofit providing prevention, intervention, and treatment services to physically and sexually abused children and their families through a child-focused team approach. Call for a local listing or affiliate.

QUESTIONS RELATED TO SEXUALLY ABUSIVE BEHAVIORS:

The Association for the Treatment of Sexual Abusers (ATSA).
4900 S.W. Griffith Drive, Suite 274, Beaverton, OR 97005
Office: (503) 643-1023 Fax: (503) 643-5084
Email: atsa@atsa.com
Website: www.atsa.com

A national organization developing and disseminating professional standards and practices in the field of sex offender research, evaluation, and treatment. Call for a referral to a local treatment provider.

The Safer Society Foundation, Inc. (SSFI).
PO Box 340, Brandon, VT 05733-0340
Office: (802) 247-3132 Fax: (802) 247-4233
Website: www.safersociety.org

Call for a referral to a local treatment provider (M-F, 9:00 a.m. – 4:30 p.m. EST). Also provides services and publications for youth with sexual behavior problems, adult offenders, their families, survivors, treatment providers, and mandated reporters. Call for a free catalogue.

Sex Abuse Treatment Alliance (SATA).
PO Box 1191, Okemos, MI 48805-1191
Office: (517) 482-2085 or (517) 372-8207
Email: help@satasort.org,
Website: www.satasort.org

Provides a network of support for abusers who are currently in treatment and a newsletter on current issues for sexual abusers and answers general questions about sex offender treatment.

RESOURCES FOR PARENTS:

The Sexual Abuse of Children: A Comprehensive Guide to Current Knowledge and Intervention Strategies. Jeffrey J. Haugaard, N. Dickon Reppucci Jossey-Bass Inc., Publishers / March 1989

Childhood Sexual Abuse: Developmental Effects Across the Lifespan. F. Felicia Ferrara. Wadsworth Publishing Company / November 2001

Stop Child Molestation Book. G. Abel, M.D., and Nora Harlow. Xlibris Corporation / December 2001

Protect Your Child from Sexual Abuse/Incest Perpetrators. Dorothy M. Neddermeyer. Genesis Consultants Inc / August 1995

Spoilsports: Understanding and Preventing Sexual Exploitation in Sport. Celia Brackenridge. Routledge / July 2001

ChildHood: It Should Not Hurt. Claire R. Reeves. LTI Publishing / August 2003
www.childhooditshouldnothurt.com

Identifying Child Molesters: Preventing Child Sexual Abuse by Recognizing the Patterns of the Offenders. Carla Van Dam. Haworth Press / August 2002

Who's to Blame?: Child Sexual Abuse and Non-Offending Mothers. Betty Joyce Carter. University of Toronto Press / August 1999

Predators: Pedophiles, Rapists, and Other Sex Offenders: Who They Are, How They Operate, and How We Can Protect Ourselves and Our Children. Anna C. Salter. Basic Books / March 2003

Protecting the Gift: Keeping Children and Teenagers Safe (and Parents Sane). Gavin De Becker Dell / May 2000

RESOURCES FOR CHILDREN:

The Right Touch: A Read-Aloud Story to Help Prevent Child Sexual Abuse. Sandy Kleven, Jody Lynn Bergsma (Illustrator). Illumination Arts Publishing Company, Incorporated / March 1998

A Very Touching Book...for Little People and for Big People. Jan Hindman. Alexandria Associates / July 1983

My Body Is Private. Linda Walvoord Girard, Rodney Pate. Albert Whitman & Co; Reprint Edition / September 1992

It's My Body. Lory Freeman. Parenting Press / May 1984

Telling Isn't Tattling. Kathryn Hammerseng. Parenting Press / May 1996

Your Body Belongs to You. Cornelia Spelman. Albert Whitman & Co / April 2000

When I Was Little Like You. Jane Porett. Child Welfare League / July 2000

Kisses From Dolce: A Book for Children About Trusting and Telling. Susan Komisar Hausman. Trafford Publishing / January 2009

Endnotes

CHAPTER ONE NOTES:

[i] *The New American standard bible* (updated ed.). (1995). Anaheim, CA: Foundation Publications.

[ii] Conte, John R. (1986). *A look at child sexual abuse.* Chicago, IL: National Committee for Prevention of Child Abuse.

[iii] Generation FIVE. (2009). 5 Nov. 2009 <http://www.generationfive.org>.

CHAPTER TWO NOTES:

[iv] "Epidemic." (2004). *The American Heritage® dictionary of the English language* (4th ed.). Boston, MA: Houghton Mifflin Company.

[v] Freeman-Longo, R., & Blanchard, G. (1998). *Sexual abuse in America: Epidemic of the 21st century.* Brandon, VT: Safer Society Press.

[vi] Snyder, H. N. (2000). *Sexual assault of young children a reported to law enforcement: Victim, incident, and offender characteristics.* Washington, DC: U.S. Department of Justice, National Center for Juvenile Justice.

[vii] Finkelhor, David et al. (1986). *A sourcebook on child sexual abuse.* Newbury Park, CA: Sage Publications, 1986.

[viii] Advocates for Youth. (2010). *Child sexual abuse: An overview.* http://www.advocatesforyouth.org/index.php.

[ix] Abel, G., & Harlow, N. (2001). *The Stop child molestation book.* Bloomington, IN: Xlibris Corporation.

Elliot, M., Browne, K., & Kilcoyne, J. (1995). *Child sexual abuse prevention: What offenders tell us. Child Abuse & Neglect, 5, 579–594.*

Kilpatrick, D., Saunders, B. W., & Smith, D. (2003).

Youth victimization: Prevalence and implications. Washington, DC: U.S. Department of Justice, National Institute of Justice Report.

Snyder, H. N. (2000). *Sexual assault of young children as reported to law enforcement: Victim, incident, and offender characteristics.* Washington, DC: U.S. Department of Justice, National Center for Juvenile Justice.

Simpson, C., Odor, R., & Masho, S. (2004, August). *Childhood sexual assault victimization in Virginia.* Center for Injury & Violence Prevention. Virginia Department of Health.

Abel, G., Becker, J., Mittelman, M., Cunningham-Rathner, J., Rouleau, J., & Murphy, W. (1987). Self-reported sex crimes on non-incarcerated paraphiliacs. *Journal of Interpersonal Violence*, 2(1), 3–25.

[x] National Center for Health Statistics. (2002).

[xi] Abel, G., & Harlow, N. (2001). *The stop child molestation book.* Bloomington, IN: Xlibris Corporation.

Elliot, M., Browne, K., & Kilcoyne, J. (1995). Child sexual abuse prevention: What offenders tell us. *Child Abuse & Neglect*, 5, 579–594.

Kilpatrick, D., Saunders, B. W., & Smith, D. (2003). *Youth victimization: Prevalence and implications.* Washington, DC: US. Department of Justice, National Institute of Justice Report.

Simpson, C., Odor, R., & Masho, S. (2004, August). *Childhood sexual assault victimization in Virginia.* Center for Injury & Violence Prevention. Virginia Department of Health.

Snyder, H. N. (2000). *Sexual assault of young children as reported to law enforcement: Victim, incident, and offender characteristics.* Washington, DC: U.S. Department of Justice, National Center for Juvenile Justice.

[xii] The Bridge Children's Advocacy Center, Amarillo, Texas, February 7, 2010, as reported in the Amarillo Globe-News article, *Battling child sex abuse.*

[xiii] *Seven steps to protecting our children.* (2009, December12). Retrieved with permission from

http://www.darknesstolight.com.

[xiv] Putnam, F. (2003). Ten-year research update re view: Child sexual abuse. *Journal of the American Academy of Child and Adolescent Psychiatry*, 42, 269–278.

[xv] Snyder, H. N. (2000). *Sexual assault of young children as reported to law enforcement: Victim, incident, and offender characteristics*. Washington, DC: U.S. Department of Justice, National Center for Juvenile Justice.

Putnam, F. (2003). Ten-year research update review: Child sexual abuse. *Journal of the American Academy of Child and Adolescent Psychiatry*, 42, 269–278.

[xvi] Abel, G., Becker, J., Mittelman, M., Cunningham-Rathner, J., Rouleau, J., & Murphy, W. (1987). Self-reported sex crimes on non-incarcerated paraphiliacs. *Journal of Interpersonal Violence*, 2(1), 3–25.

Kilpatrick, D., Saunders, B. W., & Smith, D. (2003). *Youth victimization: Prevalence and implications*. Washington, DC: U.S. Department of Justice, National Institute of Justice Report.

[xvii] Abel, G., & Harlow, N. (2001). *The stop child molestation book.* Bloomington, IN: Xlibris Corporation.

Elliot, M., Browne, K., & Kilcoyne, J. (1995). Child sexual abuse prevention: What offenders tell us. Child Abuse & Neglect, 5, 579–594.

Kilpatrick, D., Saunders, B. W., & Smith, D. (2003). *Youth victimization: Prevalence and implications.* Washington, DC: U.S. Department of Justice, National Institute of Justice Report.

Simpson, C., Odor, R., & Masho, S. (2004, August). *Childhood sexual assault victimization in Virginia.* City: Center for Injury & Violence Prevention. Virginia Department of Health.

Snyder, H. N. (2000). *Sexual assault of young children as reported to law enforcement: Victim, incident, and offender characteristics.* Washington, DC: U.S. Department of Justice, National Center for Juvenile Justice.

[xviii] Abel, G., Becker, J., Mittelman, M., Cunningham-Rathner, J., Rouleau, J., & Murphy, W. (1987). Self-reported sex crimes on non-incarcerated

paraphiliacs. *Journal of Interpersonal Violence*, 2(1), 3–25.

Kilpatrick, D., Saunders, B. W., & Smith, D. (2003). *Youth victimization: Prevalence and implications.* Washington, DC: U.S. Department of Justice, National Institute of Justice Report.

CHAPTER THREE NOTES:

[xix] Sorensen, T., & Snow, B. (1991). How children tell: The process of disclosure in child sexual abuse. *Child Welfare League of America,* 70, 3–15.

[xx] Madanes, Cloe. Used by permission (2010).

CHAPTER FOUR NOTES:

[xxi] Salter, A. C. (1995). *Transforming trauma: A guide to understanding and treating adult survivors of child sexual abuse.* Newbury Park, CA: Sage Publications.

[xxii] Abel, G., & Harlow, N. (2001). *The Stop child molestation book.* Bloomington, IN: Xlibris Corporation.

[xiii] Mary Kay Letourneau. (2010, January 23). *Wikipedia, The Free Encyclopedia.* Retrieved February 7, 2010, from http://en.wikipedia.org/w/index.php?title=Mary_Kay_Letourneau&oldid=339451212.

CHAPTER FIVE NOTES:

[xiv] Abel, G., & Harlow, N. (2001). *The stop child molestation book.* Bloomington, IN: Xlibris Corporation.

CHAPTER SIX NOTES:

[xv] The Bridge Children's Advocacy Center, Amarillo, Texas. (2010). Used with permission.

CHAPTER SEVEN NOTES:

[xvi] Bennett, G. (2007, December 13). Logic behind sex offender bans often based on myth. *Amarillo Globe News.*

[xvii] *Seven steps to protecting our children.* (2009, December 12). Retrieved with permission from http://www.darknesstolight.com.